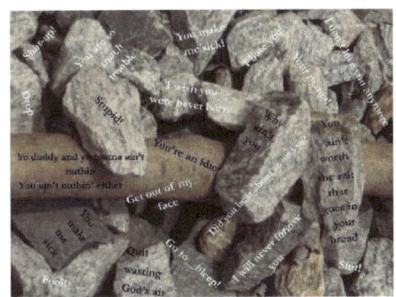

STICKS AND STONES MAY

The Power of Words

"The tongue (words) has great potential for good or evil. Those who love to use it a lot, especially negatively, must be prepared to take the consequences."

Minister Joyce A. Williams

Sticks and Stones *May*
The Power of Words

Written by Minister Joyce Williams

****Thank you Evangelist Tená Williams for allowing me to use your image in my book. We are aware that you do not spew words out toward anyone, in any fashion. The Lord bless you real good. Mommy.

Copyright © 2015 Minister Joyce Williams

All rights reserved.

All Scriptures were taken from the King James Version Bible

ISBN:-13:978-0692471746 (Minister Joyce Williams)

ISBN-10:069247174X

DEDICATION

To my beloved husband of thirty-seven years-who I am proud to also call, "Pastor", I dedicate this book to you.

You have provided many blessings for our home and for my life. Your life has covered me as you have allowed God to cover you. However, I want to specifically point out that being tired and yet walking in the rain, you did what you always do, you denied yourself for the sake of my well-being, went out to get the pictures for me that I could use in my book. Thank you for sharing your gifts of photography. Speaking clearly, your photos helped me in completing my assignment in teaching this lesson on the power of words (I may give you a quarter-lol). And your "words" of encouragement gives me comfort while propelling me into victory. I love you dearly. I pray for you continuously that God's peace will continue to minister to you and that you will receive full restoration of all that you have lost. Pastor, dear, this is the year of restoration! Receive, in Jesus' name.

CONTENTS

Chapters	Titles	Pages
	Acknowledgments	i
	Introduction	1
1	In The Beginning	9
2	Reckless Words	13
3	The Heart?	17
	Sticks and Stone Poem	22
4	To Muzzle or Not To Muzzle	23
5	Watch Your Language, Check Your Heart	29
6	New Creation, New Identity	31
7	The Conclusion of The Matter	35
	About the Author	43

ACKNOWLEDGMENTS

I thank God for my family, *which includes my church family*, Rhema Praise and Worship Church. Many of you have been instrumental in allowing God to use your gifts to minister to me. You have played a great part in encouraging me to not give up on the work that God has assigned to my hands. Thank you for your love And thank you for your diligence and for your patience. I know that you love God and that you love me too.

Pastor and I thank you all from the bottom of our hearts. Life and Favor be upon you all. We are, by God's Grace (Jesus), moving forward.

INTRODUCTION

Some teach that man is not a spirit but that he possess a spirit. Others teach that man is spirit but possess a soul. Whatever your understanding, we are focusing this teaching on the soul-heart (psyche) and it being just what the Greek word implies... *the makeup of man (will, emotions, mind—choices-intellect-heart)*. You are different from every other person. The thing that makes you-you is the soul. The soul is how you relate to others and how you understand yourself. The spirit is how you relate to God for when you are reborn, you are born of spirit. (John 3:5-6)

"I HATE YOU!" "You make me sick!" "You really get on my nerves!" "Stupid!" "I want a divorce." "I just don't love you anymore!" "You are just plain ignorant!" "You are such an idiot." "Get out of my face!" "You are too fat!" "Lose some weight!" "I wish you were never born." "I will never forgive you." "I love you." "May I help you?" Your mommy and daddy wasn't nothing and it looks like you will never amount to anything either."

Words. Many broken relationships, ministries, divisions, murders and much more have started with words that came out of the mouth (the heart). Words have power to create and to destroy. I must admit that I have said many of the words above, if not all of them at one time or another but mainly about myself. When I was a child I had rather been spanked than to hear some of the words that were spewed out at me. I remember failing at a particular task or two and calling myself the same names that were placed on me by loved ones. And of course I thought that I certainly must be what I was called, these were adults that were using these hard sayings and my goodness, they are grown and know the way, right? It sometimes felt like a lifetime of being retrained to understand that I was not the sum of those names, those words.

I am lead by God to write this simple teaching book to encourage you to learn more about the power that words have and how the words that we use can either devalue someone or edify them (build them up). Our words may even stop our own breakthroughs. Jesus said in **Mat 18:18**, *"Verily I say unto you, Whatsoever ye shall bind on earth shall be bound in heaven: and whatsoever ye shall loose on earth shall be loosed in heaven.* Amen *(*emphasis mine*). As a Believer, our words have power to defeat the enemy or open doors for us being defeated by our enemy.*

I also remember some years ago, saying to someone, whose words were causing great conflict and confusion, "if you would only put up your sword and just listen, you would get a better understanding of the situation." Of course this individual had no clue what I was saying because he was so emotional that his reasoning was hampered. Eventually his reply was, "sword, we don't have a sword, what are you talking about?" He mocked me and others joined his vicious "wordy" attack. I just moved on so that my words would not add fuel to an already blazing fire (I was feeling some kinda way, you know?). He was so emotional, so very enraged over something that could have been controlled had he and his followers would have been swift to hear and yet slow to speak. The situation blew out of control taking captive those who loved gossip and conflict. It troubled me that these were people of the church who confessed Christianity yet did had no ear for hearing or heart for peace. None of them would give me the opportunity to explain what I meant. But beloved, please read: *Psa_64:3_Who whet their tongue like a sword, and bend their bows to shoot their arrows, even bitter words: Pro_12:18 There is that speaketh like the piercings of a sword: but the tongue of the wise is health.Pro_25:18 A man that beareth false witness against his neighbour is a maul, and a sword, and a sharp arrow. Isa_49:2 And he hath made my mouth like a sharp sword; in the shadow of his hand hath he hid me, and made me a polished shaft; in his quiver hath he hid me;*

On Guard

Psalms 64 is a Psalm of King David. He was asking God to guard and preserve his life from the terror of his enemy (verse 1). He asked God in verse two to hide him from his enemy's secret plots (conspiracies) and from their evil schemes. He goes on to say in verse three that they whet (sharpen their tongue) like that of a sword blade. And those sharpened tongues aim venomous words like arrows at him. Think of that! Words. Words shot-aimed to kill! Poisonous, sharp, arrows (words) which are designed to kill!

God can heal us from words that have been meant to destroy us. But we must be honest with and about ourselves first. Remember, the thief cometh not, but for to steal, and to kill, and to destroy: But Jesus said, "I am come that they might have life, and that they might have it more abundantly." (Joh_10:10) As a Believer, we must forgive others. We are to build one another up not tear one another down. The world knows that we are Christ's Disciples by the way we love one another (Um, Oh-oh). (St. John 13:34-35)

When we use our words as a weapon, a sword (for negative purposes), we are being used by our enemy Satan-the thief, the poisonous one, to steal, kill and destroy! Paul instructs us in Rom_6:14, "For sin shall not have dominion over you: for ye are not under the law, but under grace." We are to be concerned about the feelings of others and do (include-say) unto others as we would have them do (say) unto us.

We are being used to devalue those that were made in the imagine of God when we don't allow the Holy Spirit to help us especially when in an emotional state. Of course, people can push that button, of course others purposely use words to hurt you without a moment's thought about your feelings or the pain that you may be in. But you beloved, as a child of the most High God, are not to respond in anger or revenge but in the character of Christ, i.e., love *(What? Did I say that again? Yes. Love but not in your own power)*. I can securely write this part because through Christ, I am **now** letting God do the defending through me and for me. No. It's not easy all the time. There are days when, um- well ☺. But I rely on Jesus to help me to heal from the accusing words of offenders and grace-His Love through me - as I have yielded to Him- empowered me to forgive my offenders. What I have noticed is that over the years as I have matured in the faithfulness of God, I can let "it" go quicker and more lovingly without holding a grudge. What a burden removed. Yes. Anger and unhealed hurt is a heavy load to carry. Let me say it again, I cannot do this without Christ and without being willing to let "it" go.

May God our Father, help us to be aware of our words and our hearts' motives. Put up your swords and let God heal you of poisons that have been used to destroy you or that you have used to destroy others. After all at the end of the day, Jesus came that we would willfully choose to love Him and others and real love does not purposefully hurt, kill, destroy, or devalue others. Real love-according to St Paul in the book of I Corinthians 13, is sacrificial and has restraint over emotions.

1Co 13:4-8 Charity suffereth long, and is kind; charity envieth not; charity vaunteth not itself, is not puffed up, 5 Doth not behave itself unseemly, seeketh not her own, is not easily provoked, thinketh no evil; 6 Rejoiceth not in iniquity, but rejoiceth in the truth; 7 Beareth all things, believeth all things, hopeth all things, endureth all things. 8 Charity never faileth: but whether there be prophecies, they shall fail; whether there be tongues, they shall cease; whether there be knowledge, it shall vanish away.

Defeated Are Ya? You Have Victory in You

Some of you are living depressed and defeated lives because you cannot get over something that someone has said about or to you. You have put all of your ability in wanting to please others and desiring their approval or acceptance of you and when they don't/didn't, well…..I've been there. You end up in a miserable state while losing yourself to the power of others.. You may even be holding on to a grudge and not even remember what was said or done to anger or hurt you. Some of you have been betrayed by those that you called friends. They whispered something, emailed, texted, or used some other social media to tell your deepest secrets. And now you struggle to trust or even to love again. Have I mentioned to you that words can devalue a person? Well, it bore repeating. Words are also used to control someone's behavior. Manipulation through fear (abuse), intimidation (roaring lion-I Peter 5:6-10), and belittling increases self-loathing-wow taking power over you. *Beloved, these things ought not be.* You are a child of the Most High God! Wake Up -Get Up-Stand Up! (I Peter 5:6-11)I know that what is "said" is easier "said" than done. Keep reading.

When we use words to inflict pain because we feel as if we have to get "it off our chest" or burst, then we are doing what God said not to do, i.e., do not take revenge, bless and curse not, love them that say all manner of evil against you falsely for My (Jesus) sake. We are doing exactly what Satan wants us to do, sowing discord amongst the brethren, daily accusing your brothers or sisters by opening up your mouth.

Why would you want to yield to the flesh or Satan and not to God, the One who saved you? Yes, I know words hurt and you feel if you don't defend yourself that the abuser will continue to insult you. Maybe so. Because an abuser of any type is a bully. When you need to correct someone let love be an influence in your words and choices. Rebuke in order to win that individual to the Lord or back to the Lord; not out of revenge or anger. It is written be ye angry but sin not and of course be not quick to get angry. Forgive-release-the offender. While praying for yourself, pray for them. Ask God for strength to move in the Grace that has already being given you because of the cross of Christ. *If fear and or intimidation is a factor, you may need to speak with your trusted pastor, someone that is well seasoned (by lifestyle not age) or some reputable professional help, to assist you.*

Rom_12:19 Dearly beloved, avenge not yourselves, but rather give place unto wrath: for it is written, Vengeance is mine; I will repay, saith the Lord.

Mat 5:11 Blessed are ye, when men shall revile you, and persecute you, and shall say all manner of evil against you falsely, for my sake.

Mat 5:12 Rejoice, and be exceeding glad: for great is your reward in heaven: for so persecuted they the prophets which were before you.

1Th_4:6 That no man go beyond and defraud his brother in any matter: because that the Lord is the avenger of all such, as we also have forewarned you and testified.

Gal_6:1 Brethren, if a man be overtaken in a fault, ye which are spiritual, restore such an one in the spirit of meekness; considering thyself, lest thou also be tempted.

Eph_4:26 Be ye angry, and sin not: let not the sun go down upon your wrath:

Ecc_7:9 Be not hasty in thy spirit to be angry: for anger resteth in the bosom of fools.

Sticks and Stones *May*

Jas 1:19 Wherefore, my beloved brethren, let every man be swift to hear, slow to speak, slow to wrath:

1Jn 4:4 Ye are of God, little children, and have overcome them: because greater is He that is in you, than he that is in the world.

As a Believer, you are called to a ministry of reconciliation. (2 Co 5:18, 19; Heb 2:17) You must grow in Grace and in the knowledge of God so that you can let go of offenses. You do that by reading, studying and mediating upon the Word of God while trusting that Jesus is fighting your battles. You do that with humility; remembering that you too were forgiven of much. You do that by honoring the fact that Christ paid a debt that He did not owe and you owed a debt that you could not pay. And by encouraging yourself in the fact that you have overcome every false and deceptive way because you are of God and you have overcome deceivers because greater is He (the Holy Spirt) in you than he (Satan) that is in the world. (I Jn 4:4)

Beloved, you are more than a conqueror through Christ. You have it within yourself to rise above every attack of the enemy. If you don't, take it from me, you will live in defeat and pain. You will be wearing your heart on your sleeves. And vulnerable? Yes. Vulnerable; very exposed to unnecessary attacks. Resist the devil by first submitting yourself to God. The devil will flee. Let me share this with you. I said ***"On Guard."***

It was the wrong day, wrong time, wrong person- or so I thought. I have just left the pharmacy. There are times when it's an ordeal to pick up our medicines. Either we have to endure the long waiting line while listening to complaining people, who may or may not be picking up the medicine for themselves, to having to wait on the store to put more people in position to help the customers, to finally, it's my turn. She had a terrible look on her face as if she hated me but has never had any interaction with me before. Of course, I noticed her unfriendly glare. She did not ask, if she could help me or offered any polite social greeting nevertheless I preceded to give her my name but her tone in saying "What" bothered me. Oh my it bothered me. I sighed, prayed for self-control under my breathe but loud enough for her to hear me (warning her that she was pushing some buttons). I repeated my order and she then abruptly said, "wait I have to log out of this screen before I can help you." Alright, by now, I am steaming! I looked at her, getting ready to ask her, if she was having a bad day or something but I didn't. Immediately, I was reminded by the Holy Spirit of the very book that I am wring, *"Sticks and Stones May"* and backed I down. You see all morning long I have been taking shots, if you will, from people that were hurting me with their words and then actions and their words and then actions were totally uncalled for. None of them considered the pain that was forced upon me nor the anger that was beginning to rise up in me. See, I mentioned to you this was the wrong day, the wrong time and I was the wrong person. I was about to lose control of my own tongue and advise her to look for another job if she could not work well with people. Instead the Holy Spirit led me to ask for someone else to help me. It just so happened that a pharmacist was wrapping up helping someone else and she tenderly came over and offered me her assistance. She asked me what was the problem and I was only too glad to tell her. I said, *"I don't like this young ladies tone and she doesn't like mine, although I never lost my temper with her or spoke rudely to her. However, I am sure that she could tell by my deep sighing that I was getting fed up."* Prior to the Pharmacist coming over, she cut me off two additional times, rolled her eyes at me and would not respond to my questions. I got all my meds and was absolutely, absolutely happy that I did not show myself ugly and dishonored God –though I could have went there because I felt it all the way. Did I mention that there was a couple of individuals prior to her waiting on me that this lady waited on? She was extremely nice to them even told them to have a blessed day. Lol. Yes. They were of another race. I mean other that my race. Well, well.

So. I thought it was the wrong day, the wrong time, and I was the wrong person did I? Well I was wrong. *The wrong day?* I woke up declaring that this is the day that the Lord has made I will rejoice and be glad in it; that something wonderful and miraculous ws going to happen to me today; that I expect an extraordinary blessing because daily He (God) loads me up with blessings (Psa. 68:19); that I am the righteousness of God by faith in Christ Jesus; and that I am living in the overflow (though our bills at the time, were not aligning with my faith). Bills were all in my sight and the lack of money to pay them was trying to consume my thoughts. Whoo-we! I was simply at a breaking point. *Or so I felt.*

The wrong time? No because my steps are ordered by the Lord and there was something for me and her to learn in the process of this evolving, volatile situation. That time (hour and minute) was destined for me.

The wrong person? No, of course not. Had it been someone that curses and had an aggressive tone, she may have received a group of words that could have brought her to tears or even worse. The person that I use to be would have let her have it and waited on the police or security guard to come and take me away. Oh thank God for His Amazing Son (Grace).

1Pe 5:6 Humble yourselves therefore under the mighty hand of God, that He may exalt you in due time: 7 Casting all your care upon Him; for He careth for you. 8 Be sober, be vigilant; because your adversary the devil, as a roaring lion, walketh about, seeking whom he may devour: 9 Whom resist stedfast in the faith, knowing that the same afflictions are accomplished in your brethren that are in the world. 10 But the God of all grace, who hath called us unto his eternal glory by Christ Jesus, after that ye have suffered a while, make you perfect, stablish, strengthen, settle you. 11 To Him be glory and dominion for ever and ever. Amen.

Jas 4:6 But He giveth more grace. Wherefore He saith, God resisteth the proud, but giveth grace unto the humble. 7 Submit yourselves therefore to God. Resist the devil, and he will flee from you. 8 Draw nigh to God, and He will draw nigh to you. Cleanse your hands, ye sinners; and purify your hearts, ye double minded. 9 Be afflicted, and mourn, and weep: let your laughter be turned to mourning, and your joy to heaviness. 10 Humble yourselves in the sight of the Lord, and He shall lift you up. 11 Speak not evil one of another, brethren. He that speaketh evil of his brother, and judgeth his brother, speaketh evil of the law, and judgeth the law: but if thou judge the law, thou art not a doer of the law, but a judge.

By the way, I did receive miracles that very day. When I came out of the pharmacy, not only was I rejoicing because immediate forgave the young lady after listening to God but I was almost in an accident in the parking lot But God prevented it. Oh yes, He kept me. He is a keeper and the lifter on my head.

Psa 3:1 A Psalm of David, when he fled from Absalom his son. *LORD, how are they increased that trouble me! many are they that rise up against me. 2 Many there be which say of my soul, There is no help for him in God. Selah. 3 But Thou, O LORD, art a shield for me; my glory, and the lifter up of mine head. 4 I cried unto the LORD with my voice, and He heard me out of His holy hill. Selah. 5 I laid me down and slept; I awaked; for the LORD sustained me. 6 I will not be afraid of ten thousands of people, that have set themselves against me round about. 7 Arise, O LORD; save me, O my God: for thou hast smitten all mine enemies upon the cheek bone; thou hast broken the teeth of the ungodly. 8 Salvation belongeth unto the LORD: Thy blessing is upon Thy people (Now you say-"That's me). Selah.* **Hallelujah**!

By His Grace;

Minister Joyce Williams

CHAPTER ONE

IN THE BEGINNING

What does the Bible say about words (I'm glad that you asked me that)?

> *Joh 1:1 In the beginning was the Word, and the Word was with God, and the Word was God. 2 The same was in the beginning with God. 3 All things were made by Him; and without Him was not anything made that was made. 4 In Him was life; and the life was the light of men. 5 And the light shineth in darkness; and the darkness comprehended it not.*

Let me lay down this foundation. In Genesis 1:1-3 we read, God saying , "Let us make man ("In the beginning God created the heaven and the earth. (2)And the earth was without form, and void; and darkness *was* upon the face of the deep. And the Spirit of God moved upon the face of the waters. (3)And God said, Let there be light: and there was light".

Many things in the world evolves around words. God is the One that created the heavens and the earth. The earth was without any arrangement, and emptiness: and darkness covered it for darkness was upon the face of the deep (verse 2). God looked at the emptiness, the lack of arrangement and the darkness and said, "Let there be light" (verse 3).

Now first let's notice in verse one that God created the heavens and the earth. There are many theories as to why the earth was dark, and void (empty) of light but those explanations are not my assignment. I will however share this one thought with you. In the book of Isiah 45:18 it is written that God created the earth to be inhabited (ibid). Some theologians teach that maybe in the book of Genesis between verses one and two something catastrophe happened; maybe the fall of Satan (Ezekiel 28:13-19; Isa 14-12-15; Luke 10:18; Rev. 12:9, 2 Peter 2:4; Matthew 25:41 and Genesis 3:14) and the earth became unlivable- void and formless. "For thus saith the LORD that created the heavens; God Himself that formed the earth and made it; He hath established it, He created it not in vain, He formed it to be inhabited: I am the LORD; and there is none else". The writer of book of Hebrews wrote that by the word of God, we understand that the worlds were framed-put in order and equipped for their intended purpose, (ibid Hebrews 11:3). Let us agree that even without expounding on various theories, just as He knows now, God knew then when He made the worlds (heavens and earth) that He had a purpose and that He is well aware of just what He was and still is doing. Can we agree? Thanks. The issue is that God spoke words, "Let there be light" and it was. *Immediately*!

Now the beauty of light coming into the darkness is awe inspiring. The light was made by the power of God's Word. When He said, "Let there be light"- He willed it, and it was done; there it was-light – And that same light which God willed, He also approved. God saw the light that it was good – It was exactly as He designed it (by the power of four Words-"let there be light"); and it was fit to answer the end for which He designed it. Again, I say, He knew exactly what He was doing. It was designed to cover the darkness, which can be representative of lack of or loss of viewing, or understanding. It was also designed to bring clarity to the futuristic blessings for Adam and Eve; mankind- *if you will*-to behold the beauty of the Lord and the magnificence of what He was to create for their home. Words should be used to build, bring clarity, restore and much more, not to destroy one another or one's dreams. You get the point, right?

God being about relationship spoke, "… *Let Us make man in Our image, after Our likeness: and let them have dominion over the fish of the sea, and over the fowl of the air, and over the cattle, and over all the earth, and over every creeping thing that creepeth upon the earth.* (Gen_1:26) When God speaks, things happen! *"So shall My word be that goeth forth out of My mouth: it shall not return unto Me void (cancelled, invalid), but it shall accomplish that which I please, and it shall prosper in the thing whereto I sent it".* (Isa_55:11)

The power of words has authority to create or to kill (Pro. 18:22; more on this in chapters 4 and 5). God's speaking to light to come put first things first and brought clarity to an otherwise impossible, chaotic situation. As believers, being joint-heirs with Christ, and more importantly, Christ in us- the hope-confident expectation- of glory (goodness-the manifestation of the characteristic of Jesus in us), we have been given the right, the privilege and honor through Him (Jesus), to call into existence-those things that be *not in existence* (as though they already were formed.) What a privilege! We are behaving in the character, the likeness of our Heavenly Father. What power!

It should not be wasted or used carelessly. St. Paul wrote in Romans 4:17, *"As it is written, I have made thee a father of many nations, before Him whom he believed, even God, who quickeneth the dead, and calleth those things which be not as though they were".* So then God from His love for mankind, prepared the earth for man's habitation. In the beginning, from His heart, from His love, He spoke a total of six times, a total of six days, saying, *"Let there be"* and it was. What love the Father has bestowed upon us? Who is man that God would be mindful of him?

Words indeed are tools that can produce life and or death. They were used by our Creator to model the necessity and order that He Himself established in heaven and on the earth. *Yet He never meant for us to use words to destroy one another.*

Now let's look at St. Mark 11:13-24

Mark 11:13 And seeing a fig tree afar off having leaves, He came, if haply He might find anything thereon: and when He came to it, He found nothing but leaves; for the time of figs was not yet.:[14] And Jesus answered and said unto it, No man eat fruit of thee hereafter for ever. And His disciples heard it.:[23] For verily I say unto you, That whosoever shall say unto this mountain, Be thou removed, and be thou cast into the sea; and shall not doubt in his heart, but shall believe that those things which he saith shall come to pass; he shall have whatsoever he saith.:[24] Therefore I say unto you, What things soever ye desire, when ye pray, believe that ye receive them, and ye shall have them.

In the last week before His crucifixion, Jesus still had teaching His disciples on His mind. Going through Jerusalem, the people worshipping Him as King as He rode in on the colt, He later saw a fig tree which had leaves on it signifying that it also had fruit (left-over) on it. Dr Warren Wiersbe wrote in his New Testament Commentary that *"the fig tree produces leaves in March or April and then starts to bear fruit in June with another crop in August and possibly a third crop in December. The presence of leaves could mean the presence of fruit, even though that fruit was "left over" from the previous season. It is significant that in this instance Jesus did not have special knowledge to guide Him; He had to go to the tree and examine things for Himself"* (qtd. in E-sword.net; Wiersbe Bible Commentary: New Testament).

Hungry, Jesus went over to the fig tree and found it was barren of fruit. He curse the tree by saying, "No man eat fruit of thee hereafter forever" (ibid verse 13). He saw the nation Israel (and many of us) as the tree-professing (leaves) but not possessing fruit (no fruit for God! Image that!). This recording is the only miracle (yes miracle-even so) in which Christ cursed rather than blessed, destroyed life rather than restoring it.

Jesus answered and said unto it (the tree), as if the tree had asked a question. Wow. Get this now. The tree *spoke* loudly by showing leaves- at that time of the season the figs should have also been present. So it bragged of something that it was not-complete, ready, useful. However it was not the case. Jesus answered the tree showing leaves by saying, "you will never again have a chance to fool anyone that is hungry-You will never again talk high but live low-you shall die from this moment on and never again live a life of uselessness." **Ouchy-Wow!** Now beloved, there are many lessons in this lesson of the barrenness fig tree and I really want to teach them here but I am persuaded that - it is not my assignment but I will direct your attention to St. John 15:1-10.

Jesus' disciples heard (faith comes by hearing and hearing by the Word of God-Romans 10:17) what He had just said to the tree and I'm sure marveled (though the word marveled is not recorded in scripture). *Mark 11:19-26 And when even was come, He went out of the city.* ^{20} *And in the morning, as they passed by, they saw the fig tree dried up from the roots.* ^{21} *And Peter calling to remembrance saith unto Him, Master, behold, the fig tree which Thou cursedst is withered away.*^{22} *And Jesus answering saith unto them, Have faith in God.*^{23} *For verily I say unto you, That whosoever shall say unto this mountain, Be thou removed, and be thou cast into the sea; and shall not doubt in his heart, but shall believe that those things which he saith shall come to pass; he shall have whatsoever he saith.*^{24} *Therefore I say unto you, What things soever ye desire, when ye pray, believe that ye receive them, and ye shall have them.*^{25} *And when ye stand praying, forgive, if ye have ought against any: that your Father also which is in heaven may forgive you your trespasses.*^{26} *But if ye do not forgive, neither will your Father which is in heaven forgive your trespasses.*

On the way out of Jerusalem, in the early morning, Jesus and His disciples went by that same fig tree and they saw that it was dried up from the roots. Peter seemed surprised or astounded, spoke out saying, "Master, look! The fig tree that You cursed is withered away." I love Jesus' response. He did not only answer Peter but His response was for all of them and us-"Have faith in God. For surely, I guarantee to whosoever shall say--------shall say (emphasis mine), unto this mountain (there was a mountain that He could literally point at), Be thou removed, and be thou cast into the sea; and shall not doubt in his heart, but shall believe that those things which he saith (emphasis mine) shall come to pass, he shall have whatsoever he saith." (St. Mark 11:21-23).

Recall how many times Jesus instructed them about the power of words and the authority of faith in God; I **say** (1)- whosoever shall **say** (2); which he **saith** (3); shall have whatsoever he **saith** (4). If the disciples as well as you and I, have (Gk echo-meaning "must needs" to hold-possession) faith in God, then, we can deal with the problem of fruitlessness, and remove mountainous obstacles. Faith will lead one into confessing or **speaking** boldly the promises of God. Words can produce fruit or words can cause barrenness. If we have a living relation with the Holy Spirit, He will assure us of the faithfulness of God and our words will reflect that relationship.

CHAPTER TWO

RECKLESS WORDS

What does the Bible say about words (I'm glad that you asked me that)? Answer: Words are a matter of what's in our hearts. No? Follow me.

As an adolescent some of us may have said in defense of some harsh words directed at us, *"Sticks and stones may break my bones but words will never hurt me"* (knowing all alone that we were consumed with pain). Sounds familiar? How many of you know that this statement is a lie? In first Corinthians 13:11, St. Paul wrote, "When I was a child, I spoke as a child; I understood as a child, I thought as a child: but when I became a man, I put away childish things."

Beloved, let me ask you a question. Can words hurt? I hope you answered, Yes. What St. Paul penned down under the inspiration of the Holy Spirit, is meant for both male and female adults. As adults, as "grown-ups" or *hopefully* "mentally matured" ones, we should have gained knowledge down through the years that our words can either build up or tear down an individual, ministry, church, country, preacher, children, relationships and much more. It is written in the book of Proverbs 18:21 "Death and life are in the power of the tongue (words); and they that love it shall eat the fruit of it." Which is to say, the tongue (words) has great potential for good or evil. Those who love to use it a lot, especially negatively, must be prepared to take the consequences. ***Ouchy-Wow!***

The meaning of words influences human behavior. In fact, the Bible says, Pro 12:18 "There is that speaketh like the piercings of a sword: but the tongue of the wise *is* health". Meaning reckless words pierce like a sword, but the tongue of the wise brings healing. When we are not careful of words we utter, (and they cannot be taken back as if we never said them), we are indirectly giving what we say permission to either bless, encourage, heal or run amok. It is absolutely important and necessary especially, as a child of the Most High God, that we allow the Holy Spirit, by getting out of His way, to do a work in us and direct our speech. When we do that as our heart is changing, maturing, the Holy Spirit will help us bridle (control-put a muzzle on) our tongue (words).

One of the ways we do this, is to learn of Christ and follow His pattern (more on this latter), and by willfully and humbly submitting to His will. We then are releasing our all to His control (with confident trust in God's ability to heal the hurt of the thrown sticks and stones). You are releasing control to He that is LORD. Beloved, we are blessed with two ears but one mouth. Let us be swift to hear and slow to speak, and slow to wrath (James 1:19). Let us build up one another and not destroy one another. **And by the way, Sticks and Stones *May* hurt but words-yes, yes, yes; words can and do hurt too.**

I love to sing. I am an ordained assistant pastor and teacher of God's Word (very humbly stated). I am not bragging, God forbid but I am setting up a foundation so that you will understand the following. There were seasons in my ministry when I use to sing (I only sing gospel or inspirational songs), and there were many times that I would sing out of my heart (my soul-emotions-more on the heart in the next chapter) and it was full of hurt, a anger, self-loathing, self-condemnation or disappointment. Although I was not aiming my words at individuals, I am sure I shot a few and brought them some form of harm causing them and myself barrenness. As I increased my fellowship with God through Jesus, my eyes, my understanding were opened to the fact that I was slinging some stones with my words through music or teaching or preaching. Oh my. I was hurting and my words, through whichever device, were coming out of my hurt heart (soul) and were hurting others instead of glorying (magnifying) Jesus and leading them into a deeper revelation of who Jesus was/is and the sacrifices and provisions that He made for them through His death, burial and resurrection.

When my eyes were opened to the truth of my ministry, I changed but not on my own accord. Now, I have been a believer for more than thirty-four years and preaching for twenty-eight years yet I have now- in the past few years received healing from excruciating pains including some words that were meant to destroy and kill me (my influence-well-maybe physically too). I realized that I was wearing my heart on my sleeves. Easy to offend. I took many acts and words of hatred against me very personally. I was the type of person that wanted to be liked and accepted by all people. But how many of you know that my personality set me up for many hurts and vulnerabilities?

The old man? Yes I was a new creation but I had to work out my own salvation with fear and trembling. (Php 2:12)

So how did I receive my deliverances? I'm glad that you asked me that too. I dug deeper into the Word of God. I began to confess more and more that I am the righteousness of God by faith through Christ Jesus. I started loving me and declaring that I am what God says that I am not what people say or think that I am. I fail more deeply in love with Jesus and accepted His deep love for me. I stopped walking in guilt of failures for I learned that all of my failures were nailed to the cross of Jesus. Glory to God. By doing all of the above, I retrained my thoughts (soul-heart). (Romans 12:2) Therefore, my words were wonderfully different. I was being transformed by the renewing of my mind (heart) and proving what was good, perfect Which meant that through the studying of His word and listening to His voice (meditating), I was readily recognizing what He wanted from me and more quickly responding to it. And oh my what joy; what a burden lifted.

When I truly received that there is therefore now no condemnation, no guilt, destruction, or doom to those believers that yield to the Holy Spirit and not the flesh (Romans 8:1), life for me changed. Again, I was saved, preaching, teaching, speaking in tongues but was not walking in the fullness of the overflow of having life more abundantly. I was bound to people and past hurts. I became able, empowered to release my offenders, and release myself of offending. Oh Glory, Glory. Hallelujah, since I laid my burdens down. Oh Yes Sir! *(Sniffing)*. I feel better, so much better, since I laid my burdens down. Have I really gotten it all together, you ask? Listen, Beloved:

Php 3:13 …..I count not myself to have apprehended (perfection): but this one thing I do, forgetting those things which are behind, and reaching forth unto those things which are before, 14 I press toward the mark for the prize of the high calling of God in Christ Jesus. 15 Let us therefore, as many as be perfect (maturing), be thus minded: and if in any thing ye be otherwise minded, God shall reveal even this unto you. 16 Nevertheless, whereto we have already attained, let us walk by the same rule, let us mind the same thing. 17 Brethren, be followers together of me, and mark them which walk so as ye have us for an ensample.

I stopped wrestling against people and what they thought of me. I began fighting spiritual wickedness more and declaring that, No weapon (words-stones) formed against me-shall prosper and every tongue (word) that rose up against me in judgment was proven-by God-to be wrong. (Is 54:17) I learned to turned all things over to God (I Pet 5:7)-And beloved-He is working all things out for my good. (Romans 8:28) Glory to God! Daily as I study His word, meditate on Him, I have learned to expect a deeper revelation of Jesus and who I am in Him. Daily I expect something good! Daily!

I changed my words, my thoughts and my attitude and He (Jesus) through the working of the Holy Spirit, changed my life. Hallelujah! My singing changed, my preaching was greatly anointed by God's power and my teachings were full of the wisdom of God! Halleluiah! Again, not bragging for all glory belongs to our heavenly Father. Amen. I am a living testimony! Oh yes I am! He is sovereign. He is God and He wants the very best for us and from us.

So why did I insert this transparency? **Because words are a matter of what's in our hearts. No? Follow me.** Turn the page please; chapter three.

Isa_54:17 No weapon that is formed against thee shall prosper; and every tongue that shall rise against thee in judgment thou shalt condemn. This is the heritage of the servants of the LORD, and their righteousness is of me, saith the LORD.

Quick questions:

1. Did you know that the Bible says that a deceitful tongue crushes the spirit?(Proverbs 15:4)

2. Did you know that the opinion that you have of yourself comes from what is in your heart?

3. Are you aware that you can change your opinion?

4. Are you aware that if you have asked Jesus to live in your heart, that you are a new creation in Him?

5. Are you aware that your past is just that-your past?

6. Are you aware that you are being challenged by your adversary to give up or live a mediocre lifestyle?

7. Are you aware that your words can be holding you back from certain victories?

8. Do you know your own heart? Are you sure? Are you aware that God truly knows you; that there is nothing hidden from Him-good or bad? And yet He still loves you and gave and wants the best to and for you?

We may not understand our own hearts, but God does. He "knows the secrets of the heart" (Psalm 44:21; see also 1 Corinthians 14:25). Jesus "knew all men, and had no need that anyone should testify of man, for He knew what was in man" (John 2:24-25). Because of His knowledge of the heart, God can judge righteously. Please read: Jer 17:10 "I the LORD search the heart, *I* try the reins, even to give every man according to his ways, *and according to the fruit of his doings*".

I challenge you to look up Scriptures to answer each question above or get in touch with your pastor or a seasoned Believer. One that is well grounded in the Study of the Word of God by example and wisdom to help you in your search. Next Chapter, please. *Life and Favor be upon you.*

CHAPTER THREE

THE HEART?

Mat 12:34 O generation of vipers, how can ye, being evil, speak good things? for out of the abundance of the heart the mouth speaketh. [35] A good man out of the good treasure of the heart bringeth forth good things: and an evil man out of the evil treasure bringeth forth evil things. [36] But I say unto you, That every idle word that men shall speak, they shall give account thereof in the day of judgment. [37] For by thy words thou shalt be justified, and by thy words thou shalt be condemned.

In our referenced text, Jesus reminds us that the words we speak are actually the overflow of our hearts condition (St. Matthew 12:34-37; 15:17-20; St. Luke 6:45; Prov 4:23). When one becomes a Christian, there is an expectancy that a change of speech follows because living for Christ makes a difference in one's choice of words.

There is absolutely no need to argue this point but trust me, I have been in conversations with some that declare Jesus did not mean what our referenced scripture is pointing out. Listen beloved. No matter who we are or what position in life we may hold, if our heart's condition is unhealthy-i.e. spiritually speaking, hurt, angry, bitter, immature in the Word of God, proud, etc., then our words will reflect that heart's condition. If we sing, then our songs will reflect another "woe is me" melody. If we are angry with someone, we tend to say hurtful words that we cannot take back-actually-may not want to take them back. If we are depressed then our words tend to be negative. If we are revengeful, then our words will be very destructive. If we blindly look at ourselves or if we are prone to be emotional, then our words will be critical of the failures of other's more so than to our own. Words that come out and we declare, "I didn't mean that", well I have a problem with that statement. And yes, I have said it too. If Jesus is right, and He is-always, then words coming out of the condition of our hearts, were there all alone, we simply just surprised ourselves; not realizing that we hadn't dealt with something that has been festering for a while or laying dormant until something or someone ignited it.

David in Psalms 51:6 (I encourage you to study this entire Psalm) stated that "The Lord desires truth in the inward parts" and James stated that we are to look in the mirror (I'm paraphrasing) to truthfully see our condition-if we want to be blessed (Indirectly stated-James 1:21-25). In this case, the mirror is symbolic of The Word of God which cannot lie and will show up exactly what is there. And is not Jesus, The Word of God (chapter one)? Oh yes, Jesus meant exactly what He said. Out of the abundance of the heart the mouth will speak. Out of the overflow of the heart the mouth gushes like a volcano and it will flow over and destroy anything or anyone in its path.

Mat 15:17-20 Do not ye yet understand, that whatsoever entereth in at the mouth goeth into the belly, and is cast out into the draught? [18] *But those things which proceed out of the mouth come forth from the heart; and they defile the man.* [19] *For out of the heart proceed evil thoughts, murders, adulteries, fornications, thefts, false witness, blasphemies:* [20] *These are the things which defile a man: but to eat with unwashen hands defileth not a man.*

The sinner's mouth is "full of cursing and bitterness" (Romans 3:12-18); but when we turn our lives over to Christ, we gladly confess that "Jesus is Lord". (Romans 10:9-10) As condemned sinners, our mouths are silenced before the Throne of God (Romans 3:19), but as Converted Believers, our mouths are open to praise and worship, to God and to His glory. (Romans 15:6) I am quite aware that there are some Believers who are still struggling with cursing and negativity. Prayerfully, as they mature in the Word of God, allowing the Holy Spirit to teach them-while submitting to His control, they are one step closer to deliverance. *Php_2:12 "Wherefore, my beloved, as ye have always obeyed, not as in my presence only, but now much more in my absence, work out your own salvation with fear and trembling".* It bore repeating.

Of course I would ask the question, *what is the heart of man if out of the overflow of it, the mouth speaks?* First, of all we'll state the obvious: this lesson is not about the heart as a vital organ, a muscle that pumps blood throughout the body. Neither is this lesson concerned with romantic, theoretical, or literary definitions. Instead, we'll continue our focus on how the Bible defines the heart and what it has to say about it.

In essence, the Bible teaches that the heart is that part of our inner being where our emotions, desires and thoughts dwell. It is the same as the soul. (Hebrew and Gk word) Man is triune: Man is spirit (must be born-again), possesses a soul and is housed in a body. Before we continue to look at the heart of man, let me mention that God has emotions and desires therefore He too has a heart. We have a heart because God does. David was a man after God's own heart (Acts 13:22). And God blesses His people with leaders who know and follow His heart. (1 Samuel 2:35; Jeremiah 3:15) Christians are those whose hearts have been changed by the power of God; a change reflected in our words. Remember before we were saved, we lived in spiritual death (Ephesians 2:1-3). Paul describes those who are dead in sin as: "Their throats are open graves". (Romans 3:13) Our words are full of blessing when the heart is full of blessing. So if we fill our hearts *(soul, mind, thoughts, emotions, intellect)* with the love of Christ, only truth and purity can come out of our mouths. (Philippians 4:8-9)

St. Paul goes on to say in the book of Rom 12:2 "And be not conformed to this world: but be ye transformed by the renewing of your mind *(your thoughts, your emotions, your soul-your heart)*, that ye may prove what *is* that good, and acceptable, and perfect, will of God". Change will begin to take place from the inside out when we learn to train our thinking, putting our thoughts (hearts) on the things of God. (Php 4:8) Believers are not to be like the world. We are to train, renew, make new our thoughts by reading, studying, meditating and applying the Word of God to our lives. If we are not careful, our thoughts will develop a characteristic (Pro_23:7 For as he thinketh in his heart, so *is* he: Eat and drink, saith he to thee; but his heart *is* not with thee), that will not please God. Our thoughts will eventually come out of our mouth. Remember out of the overflow of the heart, the mouth speaks?

Peter tells us, *"In your hearts set apart Christ as Lord. Always be prepared to give an answer to everyone who asks you to give the reason for the hope (confident expectation) that you have. But do this with gentleness and respect"*. (I Peter 3:15) Let the power of our words be used of God to manifest the power of faith. Be prepared to give the reason for why we love the Lord- at any time, to anyone. Our words should demonstrate the power of God's grace and the indwelling of the Holy Spirit in our loves. May God enable us to use our words as an instrument of His love and saving grace. (Proverbs 3:15)

The human heart (soul), in its natural condition, is evil, treacherous and deceitful. Jeremiah 17:9 says, *"The heart is deceitful above all things and beyond cure. Who can understand it?"* In other words, the Fall of mankind (Adam and Eve) has affected us at the deepest level. Our mind (thoughts), emotions, and desires (will) have been tainted by sin-and we are blind to just how pervasive the problem is.

Jesus pointed out the fallen condition of our hearts in Mark 7:21-23: *"From within, out of men's hearts, come evil thoughts, sexual immorality, theft, murder, adultery, greed, malice, deceit, lewdness, envy, slander, arrogance and folly. All these evils come from inside and make a man unclean."* Our biggest problem is not external but internal; all of us have a heart (soul) problem.

In order for a person to be saved, then, the heart must be changed. This only happens by the power of God through Jesus, in response to faith. With the heart one believes unto righteousness" (Romans 10:10). By His Grace, God can create a new heart within us (Psalms 51:10; Ezekiel 36:26). He promises to "revive the heart of the contrite ones". (Isaiah 57:15)

God's work of creating a new heart within us involves testing our hearts (Psalm 17:3; Deuteronomy 8:2) and filling our hearts with new ideas, new wisdom, and new desires (Nehemiah 7:5; 1 Kings 10:24; 2 Corinthians 8:16). The heart is the core of our being, and the Bible sets high importance on keeping our hearts (soul-thoughts) pure. *"Above all else, guard your heart, for it is the wellspring of life".* (Proverbs 4:23)

Pro 4:23-24 Keep thy heart with all diligence (vigilance); for out of it are the issues of life. 24 Put away from thee a froward (false, dishonest, argumentative, bad, misbehaving) mouth, and perverse (willful, contrary) lips (talk-words) put far from thee.

Guard your emotions, your intellect, your thoughts and your words. They will be formed or shaped to do good and not evil. Your heart will change! But beloved, I must say this; you cannot change yourself in your own power. Our efforts may be with good intentions but…. Your efforts won't be lasting! *But we are all as an unclean thing, and all our righteousnesses are as filthy rags; and we all do fade as a leaf; and our iniquities, like the wind, have taken us away. Isa_64:6*

Rom 7:11 For sin, taking occasion by the commandment, deceived me, and by it slew me. Rom 7:14 For we know that the law is spiritual: but I am carnal, sold under sin. 15 For that which I do I allow not: for what I would, that do I not; but what I hate, that do I. 16 If then I do that which I would not, I consent unto the law that it is good. 17 Now then it is no more I that do it, but sin that dwelleth in me. 18 For I know that in me (that is, in my flesh,) dwelleth no good thing: for to will is present with me; but how to perform that which is good I find not. 19 For the good that I would I do not: but the evil which I would not, that I do. 20 Now if I do that I would not, it is no more I that do it, but sin that dwelleth in me. 21 I find then a law, that, when I would do good, evil is present with me. 22 For I delight in the law of God after the inward man: 23 But I see another law in my members, warring against the law of my mind, and bringing me into captivity to the law of sin which is in my members. 24 O wretched man that I am! who shall deliver me from the body of this death?

Paul is saying that the law (Ten Commandments) were, are, holy but they are based on mans' doing; doing good; man's working to obey and yet he/we failed at keeping each one of them perfectly. Because he (all of us) were sold into sin (vs 11, 14-17) by Adam's fall, our flesh (carnal-fleshly), our nature now rebels against what it should do. It has its' own mind (desires and wants) and as soon as it is told what not to do or what to do, it resists (vs 18-20). It presents a war between the flesh and the spirit man (again, The born-again man/woman is spirit), and it at times frustrated him (Paul's compassion for God and His love for his converts was strong as should all of the Believers be). In his anguish he called himself a wretched man. (vs 24) The war, the disappointments were like a living death to Paul. Oh the anguish he must have felt. How many of you know when your passion of the Kingdom is sincere and purposeful, you will hate when you sin? Oh no lift up your head and dry your tears. Here is the victory; GRACE! JESUS! He sent Himself in form of the HOLY SPIRIT to live in you and I! He will never leave us comfortless. You say, Praise God!

Ro. 7:25 I thank God through Jesus Christ our Lord. So then with the mind I myself serve the law of God; but with the flesh the law of sin.
Rom 8:1 There is therefore now no condemnation to them which are in Christ Jesus, who walk not after the flesh, but after the Spirit.

Victory is mine. Victory today is mine! Now you say it, Say it again. I thank God that through the finished work of Jesus on that old rugged cross, because He rose and defeated death, hell and the grave, Jesus has won the victory and caused us to reign with Him. Now, I said now, our minds (hearts, emotions, thoughts, may serve the law of God *(for what I was trained to do is always with me-vss 17-18)* but there is therefore (because of having that knowledge and accepting-must accept Christ's finished work) now no condemnation or guilt to me because I walk (I purposefully patterned my life according to /after) the Holy Spirit's leadership. Amen.

John 14:16 And I will pray the Father, and He shall give you another Comforter, that He may abide with you for ever; 26 But the Comforter, which is the Holy Ghost, whom the Father will send in my name, He shall teach you all things, and bring all things to your remembrance, whatsoever I have said unto you.
John 15:26 But when the Comforter is come, whom I will send unto you from the Father, even the Spirit of truth, which proceedeth from the Father, he shall testify of me:
John 16:7 Nevertheless I tell you the truth; It is expedient for you that I go away: for if I go not away, the Comforter will not come unto you; but if I depart, I will send Him unto you. 13 Howbeit when he, the Spirit of truth, is come, He will guide you into all truth: for He shall not speak of Himself; but whatsoever He shall hear, that shall He speak: and He will shew you things to come.

So Minister Williams, you are saying that I cannot control my very own tongue? Next chapter please. Turn the page.

Sticks and Stones may break my bones but words will never hurt me.

If I say, "ouch" or cry "uncle" will you stop?
How can you love me and at your words my heart drops?

Your words are damaging my soul
I can't make you stop, you need self-control

You think it's funny, you laugh and sneer
But I am struggling to forgive you; I'm struggling to come near

Oh that you could feel what I feel
So that you will know that my pain is real

No. On second thought. I don't want to see you in pain
So instead, I'll pray that heaven you'll gain
For only a clear view of Jesus and His love so dear
Will lift your hurt and open your ears.

I forgive you. You are released
Say what you may, Glory to God-I now have peace.

Written and Published by Minister Joyce Williams
© 2015

CHAPTER FOUR

TO MUZZLE OR NOT TO MUZZLE

Jas 3:8 But the tongue can no man tame; it is an unruly evil, full of deadly poison.

Is the tongue difficult to tame? Yes but? Have you ever heard it said, "well if you're gonna think it, you might as well say it"? I have but oh my goodness that's a lie from Satan; a weapon of deception and mass destruction. Before we discuss James 3:8, let's read, Psalms139:2-4 and Ps. 94:11

Psa 139:2 Thou knowest my downsitting and mine uprising, Thou understandest my thought afar off. 3 Thou compassest my path and my lying down, and art acquainted with all my ways. 4 For there is not a word in my tongue, but, lo, O LORD, thou knowest it altogether.
Psa 94:11 The LORD knoweth the thoughts of man, that they are vanity.

The psalmist is first reverencing God for His omniscience (all knowing-awareness-wisdom). God knows everything about us. Our ups and downs, ins and outs. He is well acquainted with us and is never surprised or caught off guard by anything that we do or say. Wow! Think of that He knows our very thoughts before they are even fully formed in our own heads. Now, does that make you quiver? You say, Oh, oh!

The psalmist said, "For there is not a word in my tongue, but, lo, Oh Lord, Thou knowest it altogether (vs 4) What has been already said of deeds and thoughts is now extended to "words". Beloved, get ready for this: God hears every word we speak-even when those words are in our head (our thoughts). So whether you say them or think them, God has already heard them. But others haven't. As we control what influences our thoughts, we will have less and less of evil, deprived, lustful, revengeful, etc. ones. But listen beloved, others have not heard your thoughts. Not when they are still in your head. No, no. You must open your mouth and let those thoughts out in order to either build or tear down. (Page 6) So, no. Just because it is in your head, doesn't mean that you have to speak it-no matter how truthful it may be. Use wisdom. Remember Love is in you-for God is love. (I Jn 4:8)

So what about the question in the last chapter:

"So Minister Williams, you are saying that I cannot control my very own tongue?"

Yes. That is exactly what I am saying. The concept of taming the tongue is found in James chapter 3 where God declares, through the Apostle James, that, "no one can tame (control, break, discipline, train) the human tongue" (James 3:8). This lengthy discussion about the tongue is both convicting and eye opening for among the things this chapter reveals about the tongue: it is a small part of the body but it makes great boasts (v. 5); it is a fire and a world of evil that defiles the whole person (v. 6); it is set on fire by hell (v. 6); and it is an unrestrainable evil and full of deadly poison (v 7), it is absolutely clear that unrestraint words can devastate ones' life, relationships, and health; not to mention what unstrained words causes others a certain type of death. Wow! It's easy to understand how Paul could say, "oh wretched man….." Let's dissect just one aspect of the uncontrolled or unconstraint tongue.

Why is it so difficult to tame the tongue?

Follow me. Please indulge me as we read each verse of James chapter 3:

Jas 3:1 My brethren, be not many masters, knowing that we shall receive the greater condemnation. 2 For in many things we offend all. If any man offend not in word, the same is a perfect man, and able also to bridle the whole body. 3 Behold, we put bits in the horses' mouths, that they may obey us; and we turn about their whole body. Jas 3:4-18 Behold also the ships, which though they be so great, and are driven of fierce winds, yet are they turned about with a very small helm, whithersoever the governor listeth. 5 Even so the tongue is a little member, and boasteth great things. Behold, how great a matter a little fire kindleth! 6 And the tongue is a fire, a world of iniquity: so is the tongue among our members, that it defileth the whole body, and setteth on fire the course of nature; and it is set on fire of hell. 7 For every kind of beasts, and of birds, and of serpents, and of things in the sea, is tamed, and hath been tamed of mankind: 8 But the tongue can no man tame; it is an unruly evil, full of deadly poison. 9 Therewith bless we God, even the Father; and therewith curse we men, which are made after the similitude of God. 10 Out of the same mouth proceedeth blessing and cursing. My brethren, these things ought not so to be. 11 Doth a fountain send forth at the same place sweet water and bitter? 12 Can the fig tree, my brethren, bear olive berries? either a vine, figs? so can no fountain both yield salt water and fresh. 3:13 Who is a wise man and endued with knowledge among you? let him shew out of a good conversation his works with meekness of wisdom. 14 But if ye have bitter envying and strife in your hearts, glory not, and lie not against the truth. 15 This wisdom descendeth not from above, but is earthly, sensual, devilish. 16 For where envying and strife is, there is confusion and every evil work. 17 But the wisdom that is from above is first pure, then peaceable, gentle, and easy to be intreated, full of mercy and good fruits, without partiality, and without hypocrisy. 18 And the fruit of righteousness is sown in peace of them that make peace.

One aspect of an uncontrolled tongue is that can destroy any church, ministry, relationship, is gossip. Other terms in the Bible for gossip include: backbiter, busybody, slander, secrets, talebearer and whispers. So then, a Biblical definition of gossip would be to spread rumors or secrets, speak about someone maliciously *(unkindly, cruelly, wickedly with malice in the heart-oh-oh-there goes that heart again)*, behind their back or repeat something about someone else that one has no right to repeat.

You see beloved words are not simply sounds caused by air passing through our larynx. Words have real power (authority/permission). And I know that some people don't care about what they say but have you ever considered that they have been hurt so badly at one time or another in their life that they too need healing from the inside out-for again, change takes place from the inside outward? And then again, there are some with so low self-esteem that they speak out of despair? Oh I know that there is still no excuse for hurting others but love-it hides a multitude of sins (faults -I Peter 4:10) and truth be told, we have all said some things that we wish we would have never said. Right? O Come on, right? As ministers of reconciliation, believers need to possess forgiveness regarding offenses and offenders. After all , someone, especially God, had mercy on us and waited on us and is still waiting on many of us to learn and to change. Thank You Father.

2Co_5:18 And all things are of God, who hath reconciled us to Himself by Jesus Christ, and hath given to us the ministry of reconciliation; 19 To wit, that God was in Christ, reconciling the world unto Himself, not imputing their trespasses unto them; and hath committed unto us the word of reconciliation.

Heb_2:17 Wherefore in all things it behoved Him to be made like unto His brethren, that He might be a merciful and faithful high priest in things pertaining to God, to make reconciliation for the sins of the people.

Now it would be most unwise for me to tell you that it is always easy to be discipline in the controlling of our words because sometimes we just miss the mark and stumble. But please refer to our previous chapter. We must accept by faith the finished work of Jesus on the cross and willingly and humbly submit to the leadership of the Holy Spirit; spend time with God in His Word, learn how to meditate on what we have heard from Him (Joshua 1:8) and then implement it. Be doers of His Word (James 1:22-25) and not hearers only. We will be empowered to live victoriously in every area or our lives and speech.

Yes words have power. This bears repeating, God spoke the world into being by the power of His words (Heb 11:3), and we are in His image in part because we have power with words. Words do more than deliver information. The power of our words can actually destroy one's spirit, even stir up hatred and violence. They not only worsen wounds but inflict to communicate through the spoken word. The power to use words is a unique and powerful gift from God. Use them well.

Proverbs 16:28 A dishonest man spreads strife, and a whisperer separates close friends.

Gossip: Secrets, Slanderers (Mudslingers) & Talebearers (Tattlers)

1. Leviticus 19:16 *Thou shalt not go up and down as a talebearer among thy people: neither shalt thou stand against the blood of thy neighbour: I am the LORD.*
2. Proverbs 11:13 *A talebearer revealeth secrets: but he that is of a faithful spirit concealeth the matter.*
3. Proverbs 20:19 *He that goeth about as a talebearer revealeth secrets: therefore meddle not with him that flattereth with his lips.*
4. Proverbs 26:20-23 *Where no wood is, there the fire goeth out: so where there is no talebearer, the strife ceaseth. 21 As coals are to burning coals, and wood to fire; so is a contentious man to kindle strife. 23 Burning lips and a wicked heart are like a potsherd covered with silver dross.*
5. Jeremiah 6:28 *They are all grievous revolters, walking with slanders: they are brass and iron; they are all corrupters.*
6. Jeremiah 9:4 *Take ye heed every one of his neighbor, and trust ye not in any brother: for every brother will utterly supplant, and every neighbor will walk with slanders.*

Deceit, Backbiting, Busybodies, Malicious Gossips & Whisperers

1. **Psalms 41:7** *All who hate me whisper together about me; they imagine the worst for me.*
2. **Proverbs 25:23** *The north wind brings forth rain, and a backbiting tongue, angry looks.*
3. **Romans 1:28-32** *And since they did not see fit to acknowledge God, God gave them up to a debased mind to do what ought not to be done. They were filled with all manner of unrighteousness, evil, covetousness, malice. They are full of envy, murder, strife, deceit, maliciousness. They are gossips, slanderers, haters of God, insolent, haughty, boastful, inventors of evil, <u>disobedient to parents</u>, foolish, faithless, heartless, ruthless. Though they*

      know God's righteous decree that those who practice such things deserve to die, they not only do them but give approval to those who practice them.
4. **2 Corinthians 12:20** *For I fear that perhaps when I come I may find you not as I wish, and that you may find me not as you wish—that perhaps there may be quarreling, jealousy, anger, hostility, slander, gossip, conceit, and disorder.*
5. **1 Timothy 3:9-11** *Deacons likewise must be dignified, not double-tongued, not addicted to much wine, not greedy for dishonest gain. They must hold the mystery of the faith with a clear conscience. And let them also be tested first; then let them serve as deacons if they prove themselves blameless. Their <u>wives</u> likewise must be dignified, not slanderers, but sober-minded, faithful in all things.*
6. **1 Timothy 5:13-14** *Besides that, they learn to be idlers, going about from house to house, and not only idlers, but also gossips and busybodies, saying what they should not. So I would have younger widows marry, bear children, manage their households, and give the adversary no occasion for slander.*
7. **2 Timothy 3:1-5** *But understand this, that in the last days there will come times of difficulty. For people will be lovers of self, lovers of money, proud, arrogant, abusive, disobedient to their parents, ungrateful, unholy heartless, unappeasable, slanderous, without self-control, brutal, not loving good, treacherous, reckless, swollen with conceit, lovers of pleasure rather than <u>lovers of God</u>, having the appearance of godliness, but denying its power. Avoid such people.*
8. **Titus 2:2-3** *Older men are to be sober-minded, dignified, self-controlled, sound in faith, in love, and in steadfastness. Older women likewise are to be reverent in behavior, not slanderers or slaves to much wine. They are to teach what is good….*

Put them down! Stop stockpiling (storing). You can do this. Jesus is your strength. Let God defend you. He will not fail you. Come on. Put the Sticks and Stones down. Words. Yes. Them too.

****Thank you Evangelist Tená Williams for allowing me to use your image in my book. We are aware that you do not spew words out toward anyone, in any fashion. The Lord bless you real good. Mommy.

CHAPTER FIVE

WATCH YOUR LANGUAGE, CHECK YOUR HEART

Jas_3:11 Doth a fountain send forth at the same place sweet water and bitter?
Jas_3:14 But if ye have bitter envying and strife in your hearts, glory not, and lie not against the truth.

Our words have the power to destroy and the power to build up (Proverbs 12:6). The writer of Proverbs tells us, "The tongue has the power of life and death, and those who love it will eat its fruit." (Proverbs 18:21) Are we using words to build up people or destroy them? Are our words filled with hate or love, bitterness or blessing, complaining or compliments, lust or love, victory or defeat? Whoo-we! Like tools our words can be used to help us reach our goals or to send us spiraling into a deep depression.

Furthermore, our words not only have the power to bring death or life in this world, but in the next as well. Jesus said, *"A good man out of the good treasure of the heart bringeth forth good things: and an evil man out of the evil treasure bringeth forth evil things. 36 But I say unto you, That every idle word that men shall speak, they shall give account thereof in the day of judgment. 37 For by thy words thou shalt be justified, and by thy words thou shalt be condemned."* Mat 12:35-37 Lord have mercy. One of the lessons that this passage is teaching us is to not rebell against the work of *Christ (you who are rebelling against what God is doing in the local assemblies should take heed)*. "Idle words" here means, uselessness; words that accomplish nothing. Here again Jesus warns the hearer that words are the results, the overflow of, the fruit of, evil in their hearts. The lips will speak. If the heart is full of good (Gal 5:22-26) it will produce fruit of righteousness and others will be blessed because of them. Believers, your and my sins are under the blood. Nevertheless, un-repented and fruitless words, are so important that we are going to give an account of what we say when we stand before Jesus the righteous. (please read I Corinthians 3:9-23; I Jn 1:9, I Jn 2:1-2, Philippians 2:14-15 and 3:14)

The Apostle Paul wrote, *"Let no corrupt (unwholesome) communication proceed out of your mouth, but that which is good to the use of edifying (building up), that it may minister grace unto the hearers."* (Ephesians 4:29). In this passage, Paul is emphasizing the positive over the negative. The Greek word translated "unwholesome" means "rotten" or "foul." It originally referred to rotten fruit and vegetables. Being like Christ means we don't use foul, dirty language (words). For some reason, many people today think it is macho or liberating to use vulgar humor, dirty jokes, and foul language, but this kind of talk has no place in the life of a Christian. Paul continues: *"...but only what is helpful for building others up according to their needs, that it may benefit those who listen,.."* Now this helps us understand Paul's words to the Colossians: *"Let your conversation (your entire lifestyle-including words-speech), be always full of grace, seasoned with salt, so that you may know how to answer everyone"* (Colossians 4:6; see also Colossians 3:16).

There is a parallel between Ephesians 4:25 (lying); Ephesians 4:28 (stealing), and Ephesians 4:29, (unwholesome talk). In each case Paul is urging us to be a blessing to those with whom we have daily contact. Paul is emphasizing that merely refraining from telling lies, stealing, or unwholesome speech is not enough. The truth is that Christianity is not a mere *"don't do this, don't do that"* religion as some think. Christianity is more about relationship than even a religion (threw that one in for ya). As followers of Christ (disciples) we should emulate (match, imitate) the example of Jesus whose words were so filled with grace that the multitudes were amazed (Luke 4:22).

Again Jesus said that what we speak are actually the overflow of our hearts (Matthew 12:24-35). Christians are those whose hearts have been changed by the power of God, a change reflected in our words. Remember, before we were saved, were lived in spiritual death (Eph 2:1-3). We didn't care about who we hurt, how we hurt them or how often. Never mind answering to God; no we didn't care about that. But being a Christian-there's been a change-there's been a change-And oh yes It's because of Jesus. Paul describes those who are dead in sin as: "Their throats are open graves" (Romans 3:13). Imagine that. Liken unto open graves; the stench, the foul, the rottenness, death, worms, decay-darkness-trapped!

Our words are full of blessings when the heart is full of blessings. So if we fill our hearts with the love of Christ, only truth and purity can come out of our mouths. Yes? Yes.

CHAPTER SIX

NEW CREATION, NEW IDENTITY

2Co_5:17 Therefore if any man be in Christ, he is a new creature: old things are passed away; behold, all things are become new.
Gal_6:15 For in Christ Jesus neither circumcision availeth anything, nor uncircumcision, but a new creature.

If you are a born-again believer, a Christian, you are a new creature. Old things, your old lifestyle has passed away. The things that you use to say, the life that you use to live is no longer in existence.

I've heard it said, "my momma was this way, my dad was that way, I just can't help myself because it is in my genes (DNA)." Well, that too is a lie, a weapon that the devil has planted in the thoughts of those that are ignorant (lacking knowledge) of the Word of God. Your old nature, whatever you did or said, has been done away with, you are now spirit and soul and you live in a body. Your spirit is born-again and just as a child is born with no past, as a newborn believer, you have no past. Praise God. Jesus took care of all of your past on the cross.

We now have the Holy Spirit living inside of us who will help us in developing a character like that of Christ's.

Gal 5:22 But the fruit of the Spirit is love, joy, peace, longsuffering, gentleness, goodness, faith,
Gal 5:23 Meekness, temperance: against such there is no law.
Gal 5:24 And they that are Christ's have crucified the flesh with the affections and lusts.
Gal 5:25 If we live in the Spirit, let us also walk in the Spirit.
Gal 5:26 Let us not be desirous of vain glory, provoking one another, envying one another.

With the Holy Spirit living inside of you, the work that He accomplishes in you now produces evidence (fruit) growing outwardly which is proof of conversion and relationship with Christ Jesus. Fruit starting with love and ending with temperance (self-control of which none of the fruit is limited in quality or quality). The more you yield to His leadership and control, the more vibrant and bountiful the fruit will be. Your life will be fertile with seed and from that seed you will be rich in all things in Him, lacking nothing. This should give you a better attitude over life and all the cares of it. (study Gal 5:22-26)

Let's look at the fruit:
1. **Love**. God is love. (I Jn 4:8, 16) Him in you, as you mature produces love. Oh yes say, "_____ *(put your name here)*; is love." All of the following fruit are branch-offs (extensions) of love. Love is the key to our relationship with God. God so loved the world that He gave His only begotten Son….(Jn. 3:16) When you love someone, you make sacrifices and allowances. You want to please them, you don't want to sin, harm, or hurt them.
2. **Joy**. (gladness) Jesus said that joy is our inheritance. He took our suffering and our sadness on Himself and exchanged it for joy (gladness), which is not based on a feeling but on your knowledge of and in Him (Jesus) and His sacrifices. (Jn 15:11; 16:24; 17:13; Ro 14:17, 15:13; Jude 1:24) 1Pe_1:8 Whom having not seen, ye love; in whom, though now ye see *Him* not, yet believing, ye rejoice with joy unspeakable and full of glory:
3. **Peace**. (Harmony) Isa_26:3 Thou wilt keep *him* (or her) in perfect (resting, unified with the Holy Spirit and God's Word) peace, *whose* mind (thoughts) *is* stayed *on Thee:* because he (she) trusteth (confidently commits all his or her ways) in Thee. Now this does not mean that for every second your mind will be on God. But what it does mean is that your thoughts are being renewed through His Word and more and more they will be pure and pleasing to Him.
4. **Longsuffering**. (Patience) It is God's will for you and I that we develop or grow in patience. You need patience, longsuffering for change, to deal with people and the difficulties of life. But you cannot be lazy or negligent about growing for your ability to wait faithfully on God will be determined by your ability to endure a test of some form. Heb_6:12 That ye be not slothful, but followers of them who through faith and patience inherit the promises. (Col 1:11; I Thess. 1:3; Heb. 10:36; James 1:3-4)
5. **Gentleness**. (Even-tempered) the gentleness of the Holy Spirit in you, the God in you, produces a likeness of even-temperance

in the Believer. God's strength with quantify your strength. Please be encouraged that you must grow in His Grace-you must mature. Psa_18:35 Thou hast also given me the shield of thy salvation: and thy right hand hath holden me up, and Thy gentleness hath made me great.

6. **Goodness**. (Compassion/Benevolence/Goodwill) Read Mat 19:17 And He said unto him, Why callest thou Me good? *there is* none good but One, *that is,* God: but if thou wilt enter into life, keep the commandments. In this passage, Jesus was challenging the rich young ruler that God is the only one good because the rich ruler had called Him, "Good Master". Now we know that Jesus was good so what was He saying? He was teaching the young man if God is the only One that is good and you call Me "Good" then you are calling me, "God." He was telling him that He and God are the same. And if so, then we all should listen to what He is saying. And at the end of the day, He is saying that our relationship with Him (God) is having a relationship with Him (Jesus) and the words of One-are the Words of the other. Oh beloved, are you feeling me? When Jesus speaks, God speaks. When God speaks the Holy Spirit speaks. When God produces, the Holy Spirit produces. God in you-the hope of Glory! You have all that you need within you to live a godly life-including the production of your words.(2 Peter 1:2-11)

7. **Faith**. (Faithfulness) Being faithful (loyal)to God should be a joy to your growing in Him. Not committing spiritual adultery, not being "sometimy" – but consistent with your walk/your word in Him; Not double-minded, and not suborned. Psa_5:9 "For *there is* no faithfulness in their mouth; their inward part (heart-soul) *is* very wickedness; their throat *is* an open sepulchre; they flatter with their tongue (lie-hidden agenda)." Hos 2:20

8. **Meekness**. (Gentleness, Humility)Lowly in spirit-for Jesus is lowly in spirit (Matt 11:29) so must we develop to this virtue/character. Psa_138:6 "Though the LORD *be* high, yet hath He respect unto the lowly: but the proud He knoweth afar off."

9. **Temperance** (self-control) 2Pe_1:6 "And to knowledge temperance; and to temperance patience; and to patience godliness;…."

Mr. Warren W. Wiersbe states in his Commentary of the New Testament, said, "Just as Isaac and Ishmael were unable to get along, the Spirit and the flesh (the old nature) are at war with each other. By "the flesh," of course, Paul does not mean "the body." The human body is not sinful; it is neutral. If the Holy Spirit controls the body, then we walk in the Spirit; but if the flesh controls the body, then we walk in the lusts (desires) of the flesh. (Gal. 516-21) The Spirit and the flesh have different appetites, and this is what creates the conflict. *"This* I say then, Walk in the Spirit, and ye shall not fulfil the lust of the flesh." (Gal 5:16)

These opposite appetites are illustrated in the Bible in different ways. For example, the sheep is a clean animal and avoids garbage, while the pig is an unclean animal and enjoys wallowing in filth (2Pe_2:19-22). After the rain ceased and the ark settled, Noah released a raven which never came back (Gen_8:6-7). The raven is a flesh-eating bird and found plenty to feed on. But when Noah released the dove (a clean bird), it came back (Gen_8:8-12). The last time he released the dove and it did not return, he knew that it had found a clean place to settle down; therefore the waters had receded.

Our old nature is like the pig and the raven, always looking for something unclean on which to feed. Our new nature is like the sheep and the dove, yearning for that which is clean and holy. No wonder a struggle goes on within the life of the believer! The unsaved man knows nothing of this battle because he does not have the Holy Spirit (Rom_8:9).

Note that the Christian cannot simply *will* to overcome the flesh: These two are opposed to each other, so that you cannot do anything you please (Gal_5:17). It is this very problem that Paul discusses in Romans 7:15,:19. Paul is not denying that there is victory. He is simply pointing out that we cannot win this victory in our own strength and by our own will.

Beloved, please don't tell me that you cannot control your tongue (speech, words, language). You have a new life, a new spirit, a new nature. It is God through the Holy Spirit that gives you power, self-control and discipline. You are no longer living in your past. Your past has -excuse me-passed away. You can do all things through Christ because He strengthens you by empowering you with weapons of warfare, praise and worship.

2Co 10:3-7 For though we walk in the flesh, we do not war after the flesh: 4 (For the weapons of our warfare are not carnal, but mighty through God to the pulling down of strong holds;) 5 Casting down imaginations, and every high thing that exalteth itself against the knowledge of God, and bringing into captivity every thought to the obedience of Christ; 6 And having in a readiness to revenge all disobedience, when your obedience is fulfilled. 7 Do ye look on things after the outward appearance? If any man trust to himself that he is Christ's, let him of himself think this again, that, as he is Christ's, even so are we Christ's.

CHAPTER SEVEN

THE CONCLUSION OF THE MATTER

2Pe 1:2 Grace and peace be multiplied unto you through the knowledge of God, and of Jesus our Lord, 3 According as his divine power hath given unto us all things that pertain unto life and godliness, through the knowledge of him that hath called us to glory and virtue: 4 Whereby are given unto us exceeding great and precious promises: that by these ye might be partakers of the divine nature, having escaped the corruption that is in the world through lust. 5 And beside this, giving all diligence, add to your faith virtue; and to virtue knowledge; 6 And to knowledge temperance; and to temperance patience; and to patience godliness; 7 And to godliness brotherly kindness; and to brotherly kindness charity. 8 For if these things be in you, and abound, they make you that ye shall neither be barren nor unfruitful in the knowledge of our Lord Jesus Christ. 9 But he that lacketh these things is blind, and cannot see afar off, and hath forgotten that he was purged from his old sins.

How do you view yourself? It's a good question, don't you think? The way you view yourself makes a difference in the words you say, with the choices you make, with the relationships you have and much more. Jesus said so as a man (woman) thinks in his (her) heart (soul) so is he (or her). And remember you will speak out of the overflow of your heart, whether good or bad. See yourself as God sees you. You have a new identity. The old you no longer resides at your "home (heart) address." When God looks at you, the believer, He sees His Son and in Him (Jesus), He is well pleased. Therefore, if the Father sees His Son, Jesus, when He looks at you, then beloved-He sees Jesus-and Him in you-He, the Father is well please! Do you feel me? Can you digest that? He is well pleased with you! Not because of your works, you doing good is not in the equation. But you accepting what Christ did on that on roughed cross is the sum of the matter. He has redeemed you by the blood of His Son and now you are the righteousness of God through faith in Christ Jesus! Hallelujah! In 2Co_5:21 we read, "For He hath made Him *to be* sin for us, who knew no sin; that we might be made the righteousness of God in Him. Oh yes sir, that bears repeating. "For He hath made Him *to be* sin for us, who knew no sin; that we might be made the righteousness of God in Him. God loves you so much! It's an unconditional love. It's a present love. It's a compassionate love. It's an on-time love. It's an ALWAYS love. It's a present love. You say Amen. Now, now, you need to learn to love you (a healthy love) and when you do that out of your belly will flow a view of an overcoming you, words from the healed you, from the new you (*watch out world*), from the restored you; from the stronger you; the loved you! Oh may our Father open your eyes to see yourself as He sees you. He has done that for me! *Pro_23:7 For as he thinketh in his heart, so is he: ......* " What is this scripture stating? The way we view ourselves in our hearts (thoughts, soul, emotions), is the way we will treat ourselves. It is the way we think of and view ourselves. Trust me, you will not respect yourself or demand respect if you have a negative view of self. That self-portrait makes you vulnerable for all kinds of emotions-especially low self-esteem. And you will also view, think of and treat others, the way you treat yourself-if not worse.

Now to the world, the unbeliever, our heavenly Father sees you with eyes of compassion and readiness. For it is not His will that any person should perish. (2 Peter 3:8-10; Matthew 25:41) He still loves. Oh yes, He loves you too. He does not like the sin but He loves the sinner. He has no respect of person. The different in you and I is that I, by faith, accepted Christ in my life and by His grace, I live for Him; I follow Him joyfully and expectantly. So pray with me. Lord Jesus open the eyes of my heart (my thoughts, soul, emotions, and will), I want to see You, I want to see me. Save me now. In Jesus name, I want to live for you. I am tired of my old nature. I cannot change myself. I have tried but I accept by faith-what you did for me on the old rugged cross, from the tomb (resurrection), and from hell (Eph 4:8-10). Your Word promised that if I confess with my mouth The Lord Jesus and believe in my heart that thou You raised Hm from the dead then I shall be saved. You said that all that call upon Your name shall be saved. Jesus, Jesus, Jesus. Save me now. Thank You Father, I am saved. Thank you Father for saving me. I call You Abba, Father.

That's it beloved. Yes. It's just that simple. Please read carefully Romans 10:8-17

Rom 10:8 But what saith it? The **word** *is nigh thee, even in thy mouth, and in thy heart: that is, the word of faith, which we preach; 9 That if thou shalt confess with thy mouth the Lord Jesus, and shalt believe in thine heart that God hath raised Him from the* *dead, thou shalt be saved. 10 For with the heart man believeth unto righteousness; and with the mouth confession is made unto salvation. 11 For the scripture saith, Whosoever believeth on Him shall not be ashamed. 12 For there is no difference between the Jew and the Greek: for the same Lord over all is rich unto all that call upon Him. 13 For whosoever shall call upon the name of the Lord shall be saved. 14 How then shall they call on Him in whom they have not believed? and how shall they believe in Him of whom they have not heard? and how shall they hear without a preacher? 15 And how shall they preach, except they be sent? as it is written, How beautiful are the feet of them that preach the gospel of peace, and bring glad tidings of good things! 16 But they have not all obeyed the gospel. For Esaias saith, Lord, who hath believed our report? 17 So then faith cometh by hearing, and hearing by the word of God.*

Speak, words. You must open your mouth and speak (confess) that Jesus is Lord while in your heart (adhering to, trusting Him), relying on the truth that God has raised Him (Jesus) from the dead and you –yes you –will be saved-instantly! Praise God! I rejoice with you! Your words, your confession, your faith in Him (Jesus) will set you free! .

Luk_15:7 I say unto you, that likewise joy shall be in heaven over one sinner that repenteth, more than over ninety and nine just persons, which need no repentance.
Luk_15:10 Likewise, I say unto you, there is joy in the presence of the angels of God over one sinner that repenteth.

It's time to begin again! Believer, Restored, New Convert! Are you ready for deliverance; for chains to be broken; to be healed? Peter tells us, "in your hearts set apart Christ as Lord. Always be prepared to give an answer to everyone who asks you to give the reason for the hope that you have. But do this with gentleness and respect" (1 Peter 3:15). Let the power of words be used of God to manifest the power of your faith. But first things first, **Set apart Christ in your heart** (we've already explained the heart). Sanctify yourself in Him as Lord-Ruler-in and over your life. You will experience freedom and receive your deliverance. You will be growing to be more and more like Him in every area of your life (including your words). Then you will be prepared to give the reason for why you love and trust the Lord-at all times, to anyone. Our words should demonstrate the power of God's Grace (Jesus) and the indwelling of the Holy Spirit in our lives.

Summing it all up (Recap)

Words are liken unto fertilizer that gives nutrients to seed. They can produce:
1. **Spiritual increase or decrease:** What our tongue produces has

eternal implications, for it reveals what is on our heart. Jesus said, that "the good man brings good things out of the good stored up in him, and the evil man brings evil things out of the evil store up in him" (Matthew 12:35). Isaiah places words on the same level with actions for displaying a sinful heart (Isaiah 59:2-3). "Men will have to give account on the day of judgement for every careless word they have spoken" (Matthew 12:36). In and of ourselves, we are utterly unable to "tame the tongue" because it is a "restless evil, full of deadly poison" (James 3:8). A tongue under control is a mark of the Holy Spirit's power. Apart from accepting Jesus' atonement on the cross, we will be judged according to our words. Jesus said, "For by your words you will be acquitted, and by your words you will be condemned" (Matthew 12:37)

2. **Physical increase or decrease:** In order to take Proverbs 18:21 literally-that the tongue can cause physical life or death-we do not need to excise our imagination. Words create actions, good and bad, A judge or jury, by simply saying a word, can cause a person to be killed or to live. Words often save lives: a doctor advises surgery, A policeman can help someone on the verge of committing suicide. A counselor can talk with couples on the verge of divorce, a weatherperson issues a tornado warning, a pastor gives hope and warnings. Contrariwise, words can also kill: murders are often initiated because of arguments or verbalized hatred. In the sense of causing action, then the tongue does indeed have the power of life and death.

3. **Emotional stability *(or not):*** Emotions are powerful affecting, yet they are vulnerable to injury. James describes the tongue as "a fire" (James 3:16)- and who has not been burned by it? What? Lol. Proverbs 15:4 describes a "healing tongue as a "a tree of life." A much as love is an action, what would romance be without words? Encouragement often comes through spoken words (so does discouragement). Yokes are destroyed often through spoken words. Health often springs forth through spoken words, Deliverance-well you get my point, right? "Reckless words pierce like a sword" (Proverbs 12:18). The wound is emotional, and it is deep. What we say can have a profound effect on others.

Finally, God made us to be expressive with Him and with one another, therefore, we are nearly lost without communication. There are many devices that can be used to communicate, though all are not good. Devices like audio recordings, Braille for the blind, sign language for the deaf, and writing for anyone who has something to say. Indeed, speech has massive implications, especially as a vehicle of sharing the Gospel (Romans 10:14). Therefore, we are commanded to control (submit to the Holy Spirit) the tongue, to "keep [it] from evil and our (your) lips from speaking lies" (Psalms 34:13). A Christian's speech should honor the Lord: "with the tongue" we praise our Lord and Father, and with it we curse men, who have been made in God's likeness. Out of the same mouth come praise and cursing. My brothers, (Um, and sisters), this should not be" (James 3:9-10). Amen

Promise me that you will not just read the Scriptures but that you will ponder/meditate on them. Promise?

Deu_32:1 Give ear, O ye heavens, and I will speak; and hear, O earth, the words of my mouth.

Psa_19:14 Let the words of my mouth, and the meditation of my heart, be acceptable in thy sight, O LORD, my strength, and my redeemer.

Psa_52:2 The tongue deviseth mischiefs; like a sharp razor, working deceitfully.

Psa_54:2 Hear my prayer, O God; give ear to the words of my mouth.

Psa_78:1 Maschil of Asaph. Give ear, O my people, to my law: incline your ears to the words of My mouth.

Pro_4:5 Get wisdom, get understanding: forget it not; neither decline from the words of my mouth.

Pro_5:7 Hear me now therefore, O ye children, and depart not from the words of My mouth.

Pro_7:24 Hearken unto me now therefore, O ye children, and attend to the words of my mouth.

Pro_8:8 All the words of my mouth are in righteousness; there is nothing froward or perverse in them.

Isa_51:16 And I have put my words in thy mouth, and I have covered thee in the shadow of mine hand, that I may plant the heavens, and lay the foundations of the earth, and say unto Zion, Thou art my people.

Isa_59:21 As for me, this is My covenant with them, saith the LORD; My Spirit that is upon thee, and My words which I have put in thy mouth, shall not depart out of thy mouth, nor out of the mouth of thy seed, nor out of the mouth of thy seed's seed, saith the LORD, from henceforth and for ever.

Jer_5:14 Wherefore thus saith the LORD God of hosts, Because ye speak this word, behold, I will make My words in thy mouth fire, and this people wood, and it shall devour them.

Jer_36:6 Therefore go thou, and read in the roll, which thou hast written from My mouth, the words of the LORD in the ears of the people in the LORD'S house upon the fasting day: and also thou shalt read them in the ears of all Judah that come out of their cities. Hos_6:5 Therefore have I hewed them by the prophets; I have slain them by the words of My mouth: and thy judgments are as the light that goeth forth.

Additional Study
Romans 10:8-9, Matthew 12:34-35, Psalms 37:30, 31, Prov.12:18; Pro. 13:3;

John 7:38, Eph. 4:29, Col 4:6, Ps. 71:15-18, Prov. 22:17, 18

Finally, if we slander others, what does that say about our heart? We're not perfect, but once we know that the words we speak into being come from somewhere deep inside, we should start to question ourselves. We start to understand our deep and **desperate need for God**.

Ten Warnings about the Power Words

We need God's help to have a pure (and purer) heart. In the meantime, these proverbs can shine a light on where we are in our walk. *Remember the words we use reveal us on many levels. Jesus says the tree is known by its fruit, and that our mouths speak what's in our heart. (Matthew 12:35-37).* I encourage you to use another translation to assist you with the KJV.

1. *He that answereth a matter before he heareth it, it is folly and shame unto him. (Prov. 18:13)*
2. *Whoso keepeth his mouth and his tongue keepeth his soul from troubles. (Prov. 13:3; 21:23)*
3. *A brother offended is harder to be won than a strong city: and their contentions are like the bars of a castle. (Prov. 18:19)*
4. *A man's belly shall be satisfied with the fruit of his mouth; and with the increase of his lips shall he be filled. (Prov. 18:20)*
5. *There is that speaketh like the piercings of a sword: but the tongue of the wise is health. (Prov. 12:18)*
6. *A soft answer turneth away wrath: but grievous words stir up anger. (Pro 15:1) The tongue of the wise useth knowledge aright: but the mouth of fools poureth out foolishness.*
7. *Where no wood is, there the fire goeth out: so where there is no talebearer, the strife ceaseth. (Prov 26:20)*
8. *The tongue of the just is as choice silver: the heart of the wicked is little worth. (Prov. 10:20)*
9. *The poor useth intreaties; but the rich answereth roughly. (Prov. 18:23)*
10. *The power of words goes beyond you and me. At God's word, the heavens came into being.*
11. *Job_10:1 My soul is weary of my life; I will leave my complaint upon myself; I will speak in the bitterness of my soul.*

Blessings using Words

1. *Pro 9:9 Give instruction to a wise man, and he will be yet wiser: teach a just man, and he will increase in learning. 10 The fear of the LORD is the beginning of wisdom: and the knowledge of the holy is understanding. 11 For by me thy days shall be multiplied, and the years of thy life shall be increased.*

2. Php 4:8 Finally, brethren, whatsoever things are true, whatsoever things are honest, whatsoever things are just, whatsoever things are pure, whatsoever things are lovely, whatsoever things are of good report; if there be any virtue, and if there be any praise, think on these things.
3. Mar 11:22 And Jesus answering saith unto them, Have faith in God. 23 For verily I say unto you, That whosoever shall say unto this mountain, Be thou removed, and be thou cast into the sea; and shall not doubt in his heart, but shall believe that those things which he saith (emphasis mine) shall come to pass; he shall have whatsoever he saith.(emphasis mine) 24 Therefore I say unto you, What things soever ye desire, when ye pray, believe that ye receive them, and ye shall have them. 25 And when ye stand praying, forgive, if ye have ought against any: that your Father also which is in heaven may forgive you your trespasses. 26 But if ye do not forgive, neither will your Father which is in heaven forgive your trespasses.
4. 2Co_10:5 Casting down imaginations, and every high thing that exalteth itself against the knowledge of God, and bringing into captivity every thought to the obedience of Christ;
5. 1Pe_5:7 Casting all your care upon Him; for He careth for you.
6. Psa 68:19 Blessed be the Lord, who daily loadeth us with benefits (blessings), even the God of our salvation. Selah.
7. Psa_91:2 I will say of the LORD, He is my refuge and my fortress: my God; in him will I trust.
8. 1Pe_4:11 If any man speak, let him speak as the oracles of God; if any man minister, let him do it as of the ability which God giveth: that God in all things may be glorified through Jesus Christ, to whom be praise and dominion for ever and ever.
9. Mat 18:18 Verily I say unto you, Whatsoever ye shall bind on earth shall be bound in heaven: and whatsoever ye shall loose on earth shall be loosed in heaven. Amen. My words have power to defeat the enemy or open doors to be defeated by the enemy.
10. Isa 40:28-31 Hast thou not known? hast thou not heard, that the everlasting God, the LORD, the Creator of the ends of the earth, fainteth not, neither is weary? there is no searching of His understanding. Isa 40:29 He giveth power to the faint; and to them that have no might He increaseth strength. 30 Even the youths shall faint and be weary, and the young men shall utterly fall: 31 But they that wait upon the LORD shall renew their strength; they shall mount up with wings as eagles; they shall run, and not be weary; and they shall walk, and not faint.

Beloved, at the end of the day, at the end of all the teachings, allow me to encourage you to speak life over your life. Agree with Jesus concerning you.

Joh_6:63 It is the Spirit that quickeneth; the flesh profiteth nothing: the words that I speak unto you, they are spirit, and they are life.

Joh_12:50 And I know that His commandment is life everlasting: whatsoever I speak therefore, even as the Father said unto me, so I speak.

Now let me speak life over you and agree with your faith

I declare in Jesus' name that you have been bought with a price and that you no longer walk as the old man-but you are a new creature, a new creation in Christ Jesus. Because of Jesus' finished work on the cross, you are now the righteousness of God by faith in Christ. You have been made more than a conqueror through Him and you can do all things because He is your strength. You are blessed in every season. You are healed, delivered and free to live. You are whole. No weapon formed against you shall prosper. You are an overcomer and every imagination that exalts itself against the Word of God, you shall pull down! Your weapons are not carnal but they are mighty through God to the pulling down of every stronghold. You are resting in Him for He that promised is faithful. All the promises of God in Him are yea (yes-His stamp of approval) and in Him, Amen (It is so), unto the glory of God by us (God's Yes and Our Yes together-what powerful and glorious evidence of God's approval-and His faithfulness!) (2Co_1:20)

Now, you pray-Speak blessings over your own life. Say…

Father, open the eyes of my heart. I want to see You. Favor me so that I will be healed of all the hurts and disappointments that I am holding inside of my soul. I accept Your grace through and in Jesus, the Christ. I know that I have been forgiven of all my sins, of all my useless and barren words and grace has empowered me to forgive those that have spoken words that have harmed me. I now lay down the sticks, stones, the sword, and the words that I have used in defense and offense of hurt and dishonor. I, by faith, am an overcomer. I am a new creature in Jesus; the old man and its nature has passed away, therefore I have a new identity. Though I know that I have not yet gained perfection, I am forgetting those things which are behind me and pressing toward the mark of the high calling of God in Christ Jesus. My weapons of warfare are not carnal but mighty through God to the pulling down of all strongholds. I possess the weapon of prayer, of praise, and of love. I love You, I love me and through your abiding Spirit, I can love others. I am free, oh yes I am free indeed. Thank You Father for all that You have provided through Your precious Son, Jesus. Amen. In Jesus' Name, Amen.

Congratulations and welcome Beloved. Go. Tell. Confess your new-birth.

Col 1:27 To whom God would make known what is the riches of the glory of this mystery among the Gentiles; which is Christ in you, the hope of glory.

ABOUT THE AUTHOR

First and foremost, Minister Joyce Williams is proud to be a born-again Believer. She is a teacher of the Word of God and loves to assist others in the understanding of the God's Word. She is married to Alonza Williams, Sr. who is also her pastor. This union is blessed with two children who are now grown adults working in the kingdom. Her favorite scriptures are found in Jeremiah 29:11 and John 1:16. She believes in the revolution of Grace and is preaching and teaching that receiving the sinless life and the finished work of Christ on the cross will usher security and peace to whosoever will receive Him. She lives in the overflow of the promises of God for she has found Him faithful to the Word of His provisions. She proclaims that Jesus came that we may have life and have it to the overflow (more abundantly) so why not enjoy His provisions? Hear ye her.